Antarctic Expedition

By Anita Ganeri

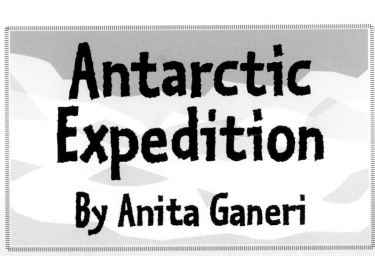

Penguin
Random
House

Series Editor Deborah Lock
Project Editor Camilla Gersh
Editors Katy Lennon, Rohini Deb
Designer Emma Hobson
Art Editor Jyotsna Julka
Producer, Pre-production Francesca Wardell
Illustrator David Buisan
DTP Designers Syed Md Farhan
Picture Researcher Deepak Negi
Managing Editor Soma B. Chowdhury
Managing Art Editor Ahlawat Gunjan

Reading Consultant
Shirley Bickler

Subject Consultant
Jamie Oliver, British Antarctic Survey

First published in Great Britain in 2015 by
Dorling Kindersley Limited
80 Strand, London, WC2R 0RL

Copyright © 2015 Dorling Kindersley Limited
A Penguin Random House Company

15 16 17 18 19 10 9 8 7 6 5 4 3 2 1

001—270532—Sept/2015

All rights reserved.
No part of this publication may be reproduced, stored in or introduced into a retrieval system, or transmitted,
in any form, or by any means (electronic, mechanical, photocopying, recording, or otherwise),
without the prior written permission of the copyright owner.

A CIP catalogue record for this book is available from the British Library

ISBN: 978-0-2411-8286-4

Printed and bound in China.

The publisher would like to thank the following for their kind permission to reproduce their photographs:
(Key: a-above; b-below/bottom; c-centre; f-far; l-left; r-right; t-top)
1 Courtesy of the National Science Foundation: August Allen (cl); Jack Green. **10 Getty Images:** Photographer's Choice RF/Frank Krahmer (cr);
Courtesy of the National Science Foundation: Ken Klassy (clb). **10–11 Courtesy of the National Science Foundation:** Corey Anthony.
11 Courtesy of the National Science Foundation: Madison McConnell (tr). **13 Corbis:** James Leynse (b). **14–15 NASA:** Michael Studinger (b).
16–17 Courtesy of the National Science Foundation: Peter Rejcek (b). **18 Alamy Images:** Ashley Cooper (b). **21 Alamy Images:** D. Hurst (b);
Getty Images: George C. Beresford (clb); Haynes Archive/Popperfoto (crb). **22–23 Courtesy of the National Science Foundation:** Reinhart Piuk.
25 Courtesy of the National Science Foundation: Kurtis Burmeister (cra); Patrick Rowe (tl, tc); Dave Munroe (tr); Zee Evans (ca).
26 Corbis: Bettmann (br); Hulton-Deutsch Collection (cr). **26–27 Courtesy of the National Science Foundation:** Robyn Waserman (t).
27 Corbis: Bettmann (br). **Getty Images:** George C. Beresford (cr). **29 Courtesy of the National Science Foundation:** Peter Rejcek (t).
31 Corbis: 68/Steve Wisbauer/Ocean (br). **32 Corbis:** Ann Hawthorne (c). **33 Corbis:** Klaus Mellenthin (b). **34 Alamy Images:** Nigel Spooner (tr)
Christine Whitehead (bl). **35 Getty Images:** Sue Flood (b). **36 Corbis:** Ecoscene/Robert Weight (b). **38 Courtesy of the National Science
Foundation:** Michael Hoffman (b). **39 Courtesy of the National Science Foundation:** Mike Usher (b). **40–41 Courtesy of the National Science
Foundation:** Dr. Paul Ponganis. **42 Courtesy of the National Science Foundation:** Ken Klassy (cr). **43 Corbis:** Momatiuk-Eastcott (tr).
44 Alamy Images: Heritage Image Partnership Ltd (br). **45 Courtesy of the National Science Foundation:** Jennifer Heldmann (bl).
48–49 Courtesy of the National Science Foundation: Peter Rejcek (b). **50 Courtesy of the National Science Foundation:** August Allen (cl).
50–51 Courtesy of the National Science Foundation: Jack Green (b). **52–53 Courtesy of the National Science Foundation:** Peter Rejcek (b).
55 Getty Images: Fred Hirschmann (b). **56 Courtesy of the National Science Foundation:** Vasilii Petrenko (t). **57 Courtesy of the National
Science Foundation:** Chad Naughton (b). **58 Corbis:** Richard Morrell (br). **61 Corbis:** Arctic-Images (b). **63 Courtesy of the National Science
Foundation:** Reed Scherer (c). **65 Getty Images:** Stockbyte (b). **66–67 Corbis:** Ann Hawthorne (b). **68–69 Getty Images:** Cliff Leight (b).
70 Courtesy of the National Science Foundation: August Allen (ca); Sean Loutitt (c). **70–71 Dreamstime.com:** Luminis. **71 Courtesy of the
National Science Foundation:** Elaine Hood (t). **72 Courtesy of the National Science Foundation:** Vasilii Petrenko (cl); Peter Rejcek (bl).
73 Courtesy of the National Science Foundation: Heidi Roop (bl); Emily Stone (cl). **74–75 Corbis:** Ann Hawthorne (b). **76-77 Alamy Images:**
All Canada Photos (b). **78 Corbis:** Paul A. Souders (l). **79 Corbis:** Epa/Yonhap News (b). **80–81 Courtesy of the National Science Foundation:**
August Allen (b). **82 Alamy Images:** M&N (cr). **83 Alamy Images:** Atomic (br); Sergey Komarov-Kohl (bl). **85 Alamy Images:** WW (tr).
87 Courtesy of the National Science Foundation: Liesl Schernthanner (bc); Deven Stross (br); Nick Strehl (bl). **88 Dreamstime.com:** Sabri Deniz
Kizil (cl, bl). **89 Corbis:** Bettmann; Hulton-Deutsch Collection (br). **Courtesy of the National Science Foundation:** Deven Stross (cr). **92-93 Getty
Images:** Danita Delimont. **94 Courtesy of the National Science Foundation:** Emily Stone (b). **97 Corbis:** YONHAP/epa (b). **99 Courtesy of the
National Science Foundation:** Elaine Hood. **100 Corbis:** Stringer/Reuters (cb). **Courtesy of the National Science Foundation:** Jaime Ramos (clb).
101 Courtesy of the National Science Foundation: Corey Anthony (cl); Deven Stross (br); Peter Rejcek (cb). **107 Alamy Images:** Royal
Geographical Society (b). **108 Alamy Images:** Danita Delimont (c). **109 Corbis:** Image Source (b). **111 Alamy Images:** Zvonimir Atletic (bl);
Classic Image (c). **112–113 Getty Images:** Carsten Peter (b). **115 Corbis:** Stringer/Reuters. **118 Alamy Images:** Frans Lanting Studio (bl).
Courtesy of the National Science Foundation: August Allen (t); Sven Lidstrom (c, b); Peter Rejcek (c). **119 Alamy Images:** Radharc Images (clb).
Courtesy of the National Science Foundation: Dave Grisez (tr); Sven Lidstrom (t, c, t). **121 Getty Images:** (b). **122 Alamy Images:** Zvonimir Atletic
(cla); M&N (tr). **123 Alamy Images:** Sergey Komarov-Kohl (crb). **Courtesy of the National Science Foundation:** Robyn Waserman (br)
Jacket images: Front: Alamy Images: Ashley Cooper / Global Warming Images cb; H. Mark Weidman Photography t. Dreamstime.com:
Yury Kuzmin / Polygraphus ca. **Spine:** Courtesy of the National Science Foundation: Robyn Waserman t. **Back:** Courtesy of the National
Science Foundation: Jack Green.

All other images © Dorling Kindersley
For further information see: www.dkimages.com

A WORLD OF IDEAS:
SEE ALL THERE IS TO KNOW
www.dk.com

CONTENTS

LOCATION

Antarctica is a vast land thousands of kilometres across, covered by an ice sheet thousands of metres deep. In the winter, Antarctica suffers the most hostile weather on Earth, with temperatures plummeting as low as -89°C (-128°F), and howling, hurricane-force winds. Apart from penguins, seals and some other animals, only a few thousand scientists and support workers are brave enough to live in these harsh conditions.

W

AMUNDSEN
SEA

Key

Ice sheet

Permanent
sea ice

Shoreline

Southern Ocean

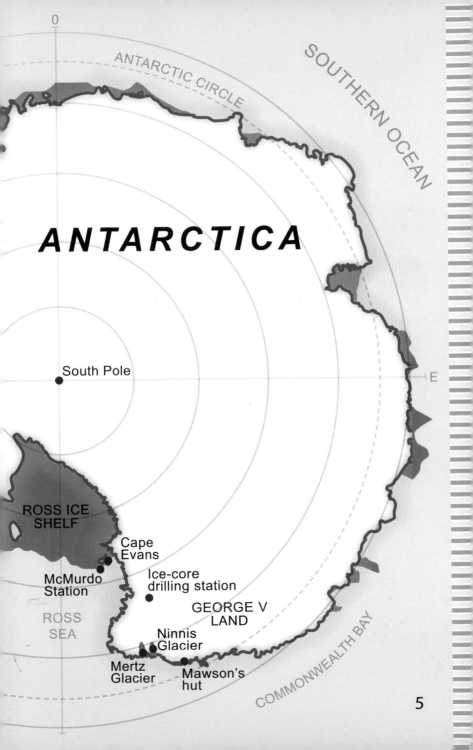

ANTARCTIC CIRCLE

SOUTHERN OCEAN

ANTARCTICA

0

South Pole

E

ROSS ICE
SHELF

Cape
Evans

McMurdo
Station

Ice-core
drilling station

GEORGE V
LAND

ROSS
SEA

Ninnis
Glacier

Mertz
Glacier

Mawson's
hut

COMMONWEALTH BAY

5

MEET THE TEAM

Meet the international team that is heading to the Antarctic ice sheet to drill ice cores from deep in the ice. They are joining scientists from around the world to take part in this project, which is called the Multinational Ice Core Project (MICE, for short).

LUCY SNOW

Job Title: geology student.
Description: has been invited to join the project from her home in the US.

DOUG WHITE

Job Title: mountaineering expert and scientist.
Description: expert climber who keeps the team safe on expeditions.

ANDY FROST

Job Title: climate scientist.
Description: studies the atmosphere to research weather and climate change.

PAUL DU BERG

Job Title: scientist.
Description: ice-core project team leader.

BECKY BYTE

Job Title: computer support expert.
Description: provides technological support for team at McMurdo.

PROLOGUE

Lucy Snow was awoken by a gentle tap on her shoulder. It was a flight attendant.

"Sorry to disturb you, but we'll be landing in a few minutes. Could you put your seat upright, please?" she said.

Lucy was near the end of a 24-hour flight from New York to Christchurch, New Zealand.

She was still pinching herself. Only a few weeks earlier, Lucy had been chosen from hundreds of talented students to take part in a three-month research project in Antarctica.

Antarctica! She couldn't believe it when the e-mail arrived, and she was still very excited. The project was going to look for evidence of ancient volcanic eruptions, and volcanoes were her favourite subject. She was looking forward to working on the project, and to seeing Antarctica's amazing landscape and wildlife.

Now she was nearly in Christchurch, the departure point for her flight to Antarctica. In a couple of days, she would be there.

The plane landed, slowed down on the runway and taxied to the terminal. Lucy stuffed her iPod into her pocket, pulled her bag down from the overhead locker and followed the other passengers into the terminal building.

Next stop – Antarctica.

↑ **ARRIVALS**

WHAT TYPE OF POLAR EXPLORER ARE YOU?

In order for an Antarctic expedition to work, it needs people with lots of different interests and skills to work together. Choose the activity that you enjoy most from each of the groups below. Then add up your answers to find out what type of polar explorer you are.

GROUP 1
A. Figuring out how something works
B. Drawing, painting or taking photos
C. Being in a club
D. Being neat and tidy
E. Being a leader
F. Fixing things

GROUP 2
A. Working with electronics
B. Playing music or singing
C. Going to a party
D. Being organised
E. Negotiating with someone
F. Building things

GROUP 3
A. Watching science fiction movies
B. Dancing
C. Giving advice
D. Keeping records
E. Selling things
F. Playing sports

GROUP 4

A. Solving maths problems
B. Writing
C. Explaining things to people
D. Following rules
E. Arguing your point of view
F. Using tools

YOUR ANTARCTIC CAREER PATH

Mostly As: Climatologist
You enjoy trying to figure out how the world works and are good at completing tasks on your own.

Mostly Bs: Photographer
You like trying something new and enjoy looking at and creating beautiful scenes and objects.

Mostly Cs: Psychologist
You get along well with others and are good at understanding their feelings.

Mostly Ds: Deputy team leader
You're a fantastic organiser and planner and like neatness and tidiness.

Mostly Es: Team leader
You like being in charge and are good at influencing others.

Mostly Fs: Radio operator
You enjoy working with machines and fixing things.

CHAPTER 1

Early the next morning, Lucy was back at Christchurch Airport. First, she had to collect the special clothing she would need to combat the harsh Antarctic weather. There were sets of thermal underwear; warm socks and thick gloves; hats; a pair of tough, insulated boots; and snow goggles. Best of all, there was a big, red parka stuffed with insulating goose down.

She climbed the steps of the aeroplane and found her seat, number 21A. It was next to the window. Great – she would get a fantastic view of the icy landscape as they came in to land.

Somebody settled into seat 21B next to her. "Hi," she said. "I'm Becky."

"I'm Lucy."

"Pleased to meet you, Lucy," replied Becky. "Are you a scientist?"

Lucy nodded.

"Is this your first trip to Antarctica?"

"Yes," replied Lucy. "How about you?"

"This is my fourth trip," replied Becky. "I love the place."

"Do you know how long the flight is?" asked Lucy.

"It's normally about five hours to McMurdo," answered Becky.

Their destination was McMurdo Station, the biggest research base in Antarctica.

"Are you a scientist, too?" Lucy asked Becky.

"No," replied Becky. "My job is computer support on the base. If a computer breaks down, or the network grinds to a halt, it's my job to fix the problem."

"Are there lots of support workers at McMurdo?"

" Ions. We're the folks who keep the place running for you scientists! There are electricians, carpenters, cooks, cleaners, pilots, drivers, mechanics…"

Becky was interrupted by the whine of the plane's engines.

"Here we go," she said.

Moments later, they were climbing into the sky, heading south. They flew over the coast of New Zealand and headed out across the Southern Ocean.

Lucy was listening to her iPod and snoozing, when Becky nudged her and pointed out of the window.

"Take a look," she said.

Lucy glanced down. "Wow!" she said, quietly. It was her first glimpse of Antarctica. Beyond the coast, the snowy landscape stretched as far as the horizon. Gigantic, blue-white icebergs littered the sea around the coast.

Lucy felt the plane slow down and start to descend. As they lost height, she caught sight of Mount Erebus, Antarctica's most active volcano. It was like being in a dream.

"We'll be landing on the Pegasus runway," Becky told her. "It's made of solid ice. There are a couple of other runways, but only planes with skis can land on them."

Lucy knew that the runway lay on top of a thick sheet of ice called the Ross Ice Shelf. The ice was up to 700 metres thick, but it still seemed weird to land a huge airliner on it!

As the doors opened, Lucy caught her first breath of cold Antarctic air. A bus was waiting to transfer them to the base. It had huge wheels for crossing over rough ice and rock.

Along with the other passengers, Lucy made her way to McMurdo Station's check-in centre. She collected a key to her dormitory room and a map of the base. She found her room, dumped her bags on her bed and using her map, headed for the canteen. She suddenly found that she was starving. As she ate, she studied the map. The base was bigger than she had imagined. As well as the accommodation blocks and canteen, there were also laboratories, store rooms, a waste and recycling centre, a small hospital and even a sports hall.

After her meal, Lucy headed to her room. She needed to wake up early for a meeting of her MICE project team. It was late, but the sky was still light. She knew that the sun never sets during the Antarctic summer. It felt weird to be going to bed. Thankfully, the curtains were thick enough to block out the sunlight.

At nine o'clock the next morning, Lucy pushed open the door of one of McMurdo's meeting rooms. Inside, a few people were standing and chatting. One of them turned to greet Lucy.

"You must be Lucy Snow," he said, smiling and shaking her hand. "Welcome to the team. My name's Andy Frost. I'm one of the ice-core analysts," he explained as he poured Lucy a cup of coffee. "Come and sit down – Paul's going to run through our schedule."

Paul du Berg, the team leader stood up. "Good morning, everyone," he said. "Let's get started."

Paul explained that they were going to set up a camp on the Antarctic plateau, hundreds of kilometres from McMurdo. This would be their base while they spent six weeks drilling ice cores and examining them for evidence of volcanic dust. Lucy couldn't wait.

Why did Lucy feel weird going to bed?

Later in the canteen, Lucy bumped into Andy again. He was sitting with another MICE team member – Doug White, an expert mountaineer.

"How many times have you been to Antarctica, Doug?" asked Lucy, between mouthfuls of pasta.

"Too many to remember!" laughed Doug.

Lucy, Andy and Doug started talking about the first Antarctic explorers. She knew the names of all of the most famous ones – Robert Falcon Scott, Roald Amundsen and Ernest Shackleton.

"Did you know that Scott's base was only about 19 kilometres from here?" Andy said. "His hut is still there."

"Scott, Amundsen and Shackleton were all brave men," agreed Doug, "but for me, the greatest Antarctic hero was Douglas Mawson."

"I haven't heard of him," admitted Lucy.

Doug swiped the screen of his iPad, bringing up a black-and-white photograph of a man wearing a fancy suit.

"This is him," he said, grinning. "Mawson was Australian. Other explorers wanted to be the first to reach the South Pole and grab all the glory, but Mawson was a true scientist. He came to study the glaciers, the rocks and the wildlife."

Andy chuckled.

"Doug loves Mawson," he said. "He could talk about him all day. You have been warned!"

Douglas Mawson 1882–1958
Australian geologist and Antarctic explorer

BASE OF OPERATIONS

Welcome to McMurdo Station! Here you will have everything you need during your stay in Antarctica. Take a look around!

KEY:

A Vehicle Maintenance Facility (VMF) looks after polar vehicles
B Movement Control Centre (MCC) manages cargo shipments
C Dormitories
D Building 155 houses the cafeteria, offices and the store
E Medical centre
F Fire station
G Science Support Centre (SSC) looks after machinery used in scientific research
H Crary Science and Engineering Centre is a research facility
I Chalet houses offices and meeting rooms
J Helicopter landing pad
K Power plant
L Water plant
M Waste water treatment plant

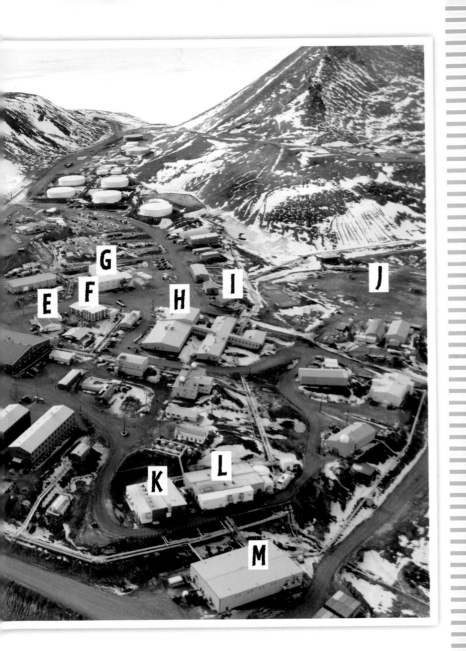

GLACIERS AND ICEBERGS

A glacier is a huge, slow-moving river of ice. Icebergs form when huge chunks of ice from glaciers break off and fall into the ocean.

GLACIER ANATOMY

Cirque:
deep recess in a mountain with steep walls.

Ice-fall:
when a glacier flows over a steep slope.

Rock-fall:
fragments of loosened rock that fall from the face of a cliff.

Crevasse:
deep crack in a glacier caused by motion.

Rock avalanche:
when ground movement causes rocks to fall.

Englacial debris:
rocks that are carried along with a glacier.

ICEBERG SHAPES

Tabular:
steep sides with
a flat top, like
a huge tablet.

Blocky:
box-shaped,
with steep,
vertical sides.

Wedge:
top narrowing
to a pyramid-
like point.

Pinnacle:
having one or
more spires
rising very high.

Arch:
arched opening in
the middle due
to erosion.

Dome:
very rounded
and smooth top.

Lateral moraine:
pile of rocks that forms
alongside the glacier.

Glacial lake:
lake formed by
a melting glacier.

Terminal moraine:
rocks that form at
the end of a glacier.

Outwash plain:
sand, gravel and mud that have
washed out from a glacier.

25

FAMOUS ANTARCTIC EXPLORERS

| Popular topics | Quizzes | Galleries | Lists |

Captain Robert Falcon Scott (1868–1912)

Captain Scott led two expeditions to Antarctica: the first was in 1901–1904 and the second was in 1910–1912. His second expedition aimed to reach the South Pole. Scott and his team reached the Pole on 17 January, 1912, but unfortunately, they were not the first people there. Scott and his team did not survive the journey home; they all died from the extreme cold and lack of food.

Sir Ernest Shackleton (1874–1922)

In 1901, Shackleton joined Captain Robert Falcon Scott's unsuccessful expedition to the South Pole. He then set out to reach the Pole again in 1907. His team didn't make it all the way there, but did get closer than anyone had before. Shackleton's most famous journey to Antarctica was in 1914 in the *HMS Endurance*, his ship that was crushed by the ice.

26

Sir Douglas Mawson *(1882–1958)*

Douglas Mawson was a geologist who dedicated many years to uncovering the scientific secrets of Antarctica. In 1907, he joined Ernest Shackleton's *Nimrod* expedition and completed the longest man-hauling sledge journey, which lasted 122 days. In 1911, Mawson led his own trip to Antarctica. His team got into trouble on the Ninnis Glacier, and Mawson was the only one to survive.

Roald Amundsen *(1872–1928)*

Roald Amundsen was the first explorer to reach the South Pole. His team reached the pole on 14 December, 1911, just over one month before Captain Scott. Amundsen and his team were experienced skiers and dog-drivers, so they were able to move much faster than Scott. Amundsen died in 1928, when his plane crashed while on a rescue mission in the Arctic.

ANTARCTIC WEATHER

The days continue to be long and sunny this summer for most of Antarctica. We're seeing an unusual amount of precipitation in some areas, though, with snow over the Ross Ice Shelf and around George V Land.

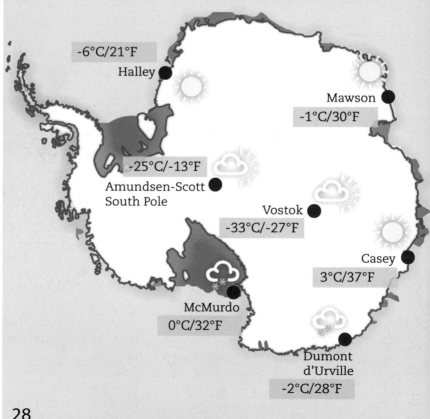

Summer Temperatures

-6°C/21°F
Halley

Mawson
-1°C/30°F

-25°C/-13°F
Amundsen-Scott
South Pole

Vostok
-33°C/-27°F

Casey
3°C/37°F

McMurdo
0°C/32°F

Dumont
d'Urville
-2°C/28°F

McMurdo Forecast

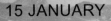

15 JANUARY

HIGH 2°C/36°F
LOW -2°C/28°F

Chance of precipitation	70%
Wind	NW at 16 to 32 kph/10 to 20 mph
Humidity	0.03%
Sunrise	Up all day
Sunset	Up all day

Thurs	Fri	Sat	Sun
HIGH 1°C/34°F	HIGH 4°C/39°F	HIGH 0°C/32°F	HIGH -4°C/25°F
LOW -2°C/28°F	LOW -2°C/28°F	LOW -6°C/21°F	LOW -6°C/21°F

Around Antarctica

Amundsen-Scott South Pole	HIGH -24°C/-11°F LOW -27°C/-17°F
Casey	HIGH 5°C/41°F LOW 0°C/32°F
Dumont d'Urville	HIGH 0°C/32°F LOW -3°C/27°F
Halley	HIGH 1°C/34°F LOW -12°C/10°F
Mawson	HIGH 1°C/34°F LOW -3°C/27°F
Vostok	HIGH -27°C/-17°F LOW -39°C/-38°F

CHAPTER 2

Lucy had a couple of days to get used to life on the base before beginning a week-long survival training course with some other new arrivals. She was pleased to see that Doug White was one of the course instructors.

"Antarctic weather can be really hostile, even in summer," explained Doug. "The temperature can drop to -30°C, and we often get gale-force winds and blizzards. That sort of weather is life threatening. Crevasses are another major hazard. Anyone who is heading for a remote field station must learn how to survive. In an emergency, it might take days for help to arrive."

The first lesson was a first aid course. Lucy learned how to identify and treat conditions that are quite common in Antarctica, including hypothermia, frostbite, altitude sickness and snow blindness.

Then Doug showed the trainees how to dress properly for the Antarctic conditions. They learned that wearing layers of clothes stops body heat from escaping; that gloves, boots and face masks are vital to prevent frostbite; and that ski goggles prevent snow blindness. There was so much to remember!

The next day, the trainees went outside to learn how to set up a camp. Doug explained how to choose a good campsite, and how to put up a tent. The tents were not like the ones Lucy had camped in on holiday. These were square at the base and pointed at the top.

"They're called pyramid tents," explained Anna, one of the other instructors. "We use them here because they're very stable in strong winds."

She showed them how to pile snow around the base of the tent to keep the wind out.

"Do you ever build igloos for shelter?" somebody asked.

"Occasionally," replied Anna, "and it's a good skill to have. Why don't we give it a try? Someone grab that snow saw."

She showed them how to cut blocks of snow with the saw, and how to build them into a dome. They all crowded into the finished igloo.

"An igloo's warmer than a tent, even though it's made of ice," explained Anna, "but as you've seen, it takes a long time to build. Digging a snow cave is better if you need shelter fast."

Over the next few days, the instructors taught Lucy and the other trainees everything else they needed to know. They learned about using radios to communicate with each other, with bases such as McMurdo and with planes. They learned to navigate from one place to another using GPS units, maps and magnetic compasses.

"Navigation without GPS is tricky here," said Doug, "because you can travel for hundreds of kilometres without seeing any landmarks. Without GPS, you'd soon be lost."

On the final day of the course, the groups learned about crevasses – giant, deadly cracks in the ice, often hundreds of metres deep, and frequently hidden by snow.

"You need to know how to spot crevasses, how to cross over them safely, and if you do fall in, how to get out again," explained Doug. "We've even dug a small crevasse for you to practise in! Any volunteers? Lucy, what about you?"

Lucy pulled on her climbing harness and roped up together with three of the others. She knew that these were skills that could save her life. If one person fell in, the others could pull him or her out. At least, that was the plan.

As the final part of their training, Anna and Doug organised a two-day trip so that the trainees could practise their newfound skills.

"Before we go, we'll practise driving the snowmobiles," said Doug.

They took turns driving the machines backwards and forwards in the snow.

Soon they were setting off across the Ross Ice Shelf – their first experience of wild Antarctica. After a couple of hours, Doug asked them to set up camp and cook a meal. Lucy pitched her tent without a problem, and then made stew by pouring hot water into ready-made packets.

As they ate, Doug told Lucy more about Douglas Mawson.

"Mawson and his men didn't have delicious food like this," he said. "When they were travelling by sledge, they ate tasteless crackers and stuff called pemmican made of minced meat and melted fat."

"Yuck!" said Lucy. "Sounds disgusting. What sort of sledge did Mawson use?"

"Almost the same as the ones we're using, but of course he didn't have snowmobiles to pull them!" replied Doug. "He had teams of dogs instead. You couldn't do that now, of course. Dogs aren't allowed on Antarctica any more because people were concerned that they were spreading diseases that were killing the seals."

Back from the training camp, Lucy had a well-earned day off. At breakfast, she bumped into Andy.

"Feel like a trip to Cape Evans?" he asked.

"What's there?" asked Lucy.

"Scott's hut. Remember Doug telling us about it?"

"Of course. Great. I'd love to go."

"Good. There's a bus leaving in 20 minutes. A few people are going."

Lucy was amazed when they arrived at the hut.

"Scott built this hut in 1911, and some of Shackleton's men stayed here in 1916," explained Andy.

Their stuff was still there. The kitchen was full of food cans. There were books, magazines and clothes lying around, and the lab was full of chemicals. Outside were wooden crates. Some contained more cans. Some were full of penguin eggs; others held seal blubber.

As they left, the driver spotted a group of penguins. They drove closer.

"They're emperors!" somebody shouted.

"Take a look," said Andy, passing Lucy his binoculars.

"They're fantastic," said Lucy. "Isn't the emperor the biggest species of penguin?"

"That's right," replied Andy. "The adults are more than one metre tall."

Emperor penguins can 'fly' out of the water to catch fish and hop up onto the ice.

PENGUIN PRISONER LINE-UP

These pesky penguins have been pinching each other's pebbles!

These penguins are not as innocent as they look! They have all been caught red-flippered and are being held under suspicion of theft and bullying. Witnesses have reported that, in the dead of night, these penguins have been seen stealing stones and chicks from their unsuspecting neighbours. Let's hear the facts.

CHARGES

This penguin has been accused of stealing rocks from other penguins' nests. Witnesses have stated that they saw him taking the rocks and putting them in his own nest to help keep his egg warm until it hatched.

ADÉLIE PENGUIN
PRISONER: AP2556

FACT: Always planning their getaway, Adélie penguins can swim very fast. They can also jump up to 1 m (3 ft) out of the water and into the air, making them look as if they are flying.

CHARGES

This penguin is under suspicion of bullying and theft. Not only has this thug been seen stealing stones, but he has also been spotted bullying the Adélie penguins out of their nesting site, hoping to make space for his own nest.

CHINSTRAP PENGUIN
PRISONER: CP6598

FACT: Chinstrap penguins are expert climbers. They use their beaks and claws to scale rocks to find the perfect nesting sites.

CHARGES

This female penguin has been charged with kidnapping. After finding that her baby chick had gone missing, she was so upset that she stole a chick from a neighbouring penguin couple.

EMPEROR PENGUIN
PRISONER: EP1489

FACT: Instead of making nests, a male emperor penguin will rest his egg on his feet and cover it with a fold of skin to keep it warm. He stands like this for up to two months, and doesn't even move to eat.

ANTARCTIC APPAREL

Good evening, and welcome to our annual Antarctic Apparel Fashion Show. Our models will be displaying some of the best in modern and retro pieces of clothing. Each item has been chosen by our expert panel to showcase designs from past and present that are not only chic, but also cosy.

CLASSIC CLOTHING

WOOLLEN UNDERGARMENTS

The fabrics that were in fashion in the 1900s were made from natural fibres. However, the problem with these garments was that the wearer got cold when he or she sweated because the clothes did not dry.

GLOVES

To keep out the cold, early Antarctic explorers would have worn woollen gloves topped with reindeer-fur mittens.

FINNESKO BOOTS

These boots would have been all the rage in the 1900s. Made from reindeer fur and with a lining of sennegrass (insulating grass), they would have kept explorers' feet warm and dry.

MODERN WINTER WEAR

THERMALS

Our model is sporting the latest designs in lightweight thermal undergarments. This inner layer is worn next to the skin to help keep body heat in.

GOGGLES

These cool shades will protect your eyes from the glare of the sunlight reflecting off the snow.

OUTER LAYER

Turn heads in this eye-catching jacket. The goosedown core keeps you warm and toasty, while the nylon covering makes the outfit waterproof.

MITTENS

Your outfit wouldn't be complete without a stylish pair of mittens to keep your fingers snug. This pair is double-layered for warmth and has adjustable wrists to prevent snow from getting in.

GLACIER BOOTS

This pair of fashionable boots lets you step out in style. The thick, ridged rubber soles prevent you from slipping on any ice or snow.

HOW TO BUILD AN IGLOO

YOU WILL NEED

- waterproof gloves
- warm clothes
- shovel
- large jagged-edged kitchen knife
- old woodworking saw
- lots of snow

KNIVES ARE SHARP!
GET AN ADULT TO HELP YOU.

1 Find some hard-packed snow and ask an adult to use the saw or knife to cut some large rectangular blocks. Stand the blocks in a circle and cut the tops so that they slope down towards the centre.

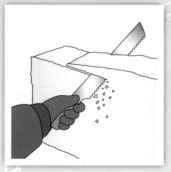

2 Use the shovel to dig out about 1 m (3 ft) of snow from the inside of the circle. Leave a section at the back of the igloo to make a seat.

3 Cut more blocks with slanted tops and place them on top of the first layer across the joins between the blocks below.

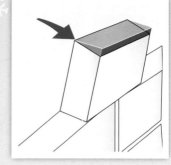

4 When the wall is high enough, cut an arched doorway into one side of the igloo and dig an entrance passageway. Build a tunnel over the entranceway.

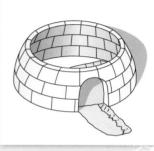

5 Add more layers to the igloo, with each one leaning further in to form the dome.

6 Plug any gaps with snow, but make sure to leave small holes in the roof to let in fresh air. Your igloo is now finished.

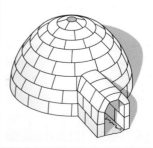

CHAPTER 3

It was time for the MICE team to leave McMurdo. They had been busy making lists of all the equipment they would need to live and work on the ice for six weeks. Now everything was laid out on the floor of one of McMurdo's aircraft hangars. There were tents, sleeping bags, stoves, fuel, food, radios, the ice-core drilling equipment, snowmobiles and numerous other items. Lucy helped check the equipment against the lists.

"How are we actually getting to the field station?" Lucy asked Doug.

"Twin Otter," replied Andy. "It'll probably take three trips with all this gear."

Twin Otters were the workhorses of Antarctica. Lucy had seen them flying in and out of McMurdo. Able to take off and land on short runways, these planes carried scientists and their equipment all over the continent. In Antarctica, the Twin Otters were fitted with skis instead of wheels. Their skilled pilots could land them anywhere with a flat area of snow.

"The pilots will take a Twin Otter out to the campsite to check that there's a smooth patch of snow to land on. Paul will go with them," explained Andy as he checked another item off his checklist. "It'll take them a few hours. When they get back, we'll get the first load of equipment on board."

Doug told Lucy that the first flight needed to take the tents, the stoves and enough food and fuel for a couple of weeks, as well as all their survival gear.

"It's standard procedure," said Doug. "Then if a blizzard comes in, and the next delivery flight is delayed, we'll have everything we need to survive until the weather improves."

Finally, it was the team's turn to take off. After a smooth flight, the Twin Otter slithered to a stop on the ice.

"Welcome to your new home!" shouted Paul from the front of the plane. "The first job is to get the radio set up and tested. Can you do that, Doug? If we can't make contact with McMurdo, the pilots will have to take us back."

Soon the team had set up not only the working radio, but also their own sleeping tents and a mess tent where they would cook and eat. They had marked out the ends of the runway with flags to make it easier for the pilots to land on the next flight.

Over the next few days, Lucy helped set up the ice-core drilling tent. This meant digging out a trench about two metres deep and three metres wide for the ice-core drill to stand in.

Lucy was breathing heavily as she dug.

"This is hard work," she said to Andy.

"It's probably the thin air," explained Andy. "We're about 2,000 metres above sea level here, so there's less oxygen for you to breathe than there was down at McMurdo. The centre of the ice sheet is around 4,000 metres above sea level. Up there, people sometimes suffer from real altitude sickness. They can get headaches and feel exhausted. Most people acclimatise to it, but some people have to come back down to sea level."

The team put a tunnel-shaped tent over the drilling trench and started to assemble the drilling machine.

"This is the ice-cutting auger," said Andy, showing Lucy a metal tube two metres long with sharp teeth at one end. "As it cuts down through the ice, the centre fills with ice, making an ice core. When it's full, we pull it up and take out the ice. Then we drop it back down and start again."

"How deep are we going to drill?" asked Lucy.

"We're hoping to get down to about 300 metres," answered Andy. "As you know, the Antarctic ice sheet is made of snow that has fallen over hundreds of thousands of years. The ice that's 300 metres down fell about 10,000 years ago."

"Wow," said Lucy. "It'll be cool to see ice that old. Will we be able to see air bubbles in it, Andy?"

Lucy knew that air bubbles in ice cores could tell scientists about what the Earth was like in the past. It helped scientists study climate change.

"We should be able to," said Andy. "Fingers crossed."

"Will we be able to see layers of volcanic ash in the cores, too?" Lucy asked.

"With a bit of luck, we'll find some layers thick enough to see, but some layers are too thin to see," replied Andy.

It was volcanic ash they were looking for. Studying the ice cores would tell them when ancient volcanoes had erupted in Antarctica. If they found a layer of ash in an ice core, it would show that a volcano had erupted because ash from the eruption would have fallen onto the Antarctic ice.

If a layer of ash were thick enough to see, it would be evidence of a major eruption.

"We're going to send the ice cores to the lab back in New Zealand for analysis," explained Andy. "The lab will be able to detect any bits of ash too small for us to see."

ANTARCTIC AILMENTS

Good morning. Welcome to the McMurdo Medical Centre. Our team specialises in the many diseases and ailments that occur in the harsh Antarctic conditions. We will do our best to treat you as soon as possible. Please take a seat, and someone will see you shortly.

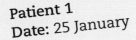

Patient 1
Date: 25 January

History: patient has been working with the ice-drilling team and has been forced to work long shifts for the past two weeks. No previous medical problems or allergies.

Examination: patient has complained that he has trouble concentrating and staying awake during the day. Patient has also experienced hallucinations.

Diagnosis: sleep deprivation.

Treatment: take some time off work and try to get eight hours of uninterrupted sleep each night. Eat healthily and drink plenty of fluids.

Patient 2
Date: 1 July

History: family history of diabetes.

Examination: patient is shivering violently and is having trouble breathing. Her skin is very pale and her temperature reading shows 34°C (93.2°F). Normal body temperature should be around 37°C (98.6°F).

Diagnosis: hypothermia.

Treatment: patient is to remove wet clothing and be wrapped in warm towels and blankets. Patient is to be given a warm drink and some high-energy food.

Patient 3
Date: 2 August

History: patient was lost outside in a snow blizzard for a number of hours.

Examination: patient is experiencing a tingling sensation in his fingers, which are also throbbing and aching. His skin feels very cold and looks white.

Diagnosis: frostnip – not as severe as frostbite.

Treatment: patient has been advised to warm his hands slowly by placing them in warm (but not hot) water. His fingers should then be wrapped in bandages to avoid infection.

CHAPTER 4

After two weeks of living at the field station, Lucy was familiar with the routine of the camp. She was really enjoying helping out at the ice-core drilling tent. Every few hours, they winched up the drilling auger, took out the freshly-cut ice core and sent the auger back down again. Each time, the hole dug by the auger went a little deeper. The team carefully wrapped and labelled the cores, and stored them at one end of the drilling tent.

One morning, Lucy was labelling a new ice core, when Andy came into the drilling tent.

"What depth is this one from?" he asked.

"Just over 90 metres," answered Lucy.

"Excellent," said Andy. "That means we're a little ahead of schedule. Did you see that layer of ash in one of yesterday's cores?"

"I did. Exciting, wasn't it? It shows there was a volcanic eruption around here about 3,000 years ago."

"That's right. It was exactly what we're looking for," commented Andy. "I'll take over the drilling now if you want to grab something to eat," he added.

"Thanks," Lucy said, and headed outside.

Lucy was in the mess tent, drinking a warm cup of coffee, when Paul squeezed through the narrow door.

"Hi, Lucy," he said, as he sat down at the table. "How would you like a break from working on the drilling rig? We need a team to repair a couple of GPS stations down towards the coast."

Lucy was eager to see more of Antarctica. "I'd love to go," she said. "How do we get there?"

"Snowmobile," replied Paul. "Andy and Doug are coming with you. It'll be good experience for you. It'll take two or three days to get there, and you'll have to set up camp each evening. You three will be on your own out there."

"Fantastic!" said Lucy, with a beaming smile.

As Paul left the tent, Doug came in.

"Heard the good news?" he asked.

Lucy was still grinning. "When do we leave?"

"Tomorrow," replied Doug, "so we'll have to get going and pack up the gear we'll need. Come on."

How long ago was
the major volcanic
eruption?

"What do the GPS stations actually do?" Lucy asked Doug, as they packed up food supplies for the trip.

Doug explained that scientists set up GPS stations to measure how fast the ice in the glaciers is sliding along.

"The stations automatically radio their position to base every day. A station measures its position to the nearest centimetre. It's a hundred times more accurate than the GPS on your phone or in your car."

Doug picked up a map from the pile of equipment. "I'll show you where we're going," he said, unfolding the map on the floor.

"We're here at the moment," he said, pointing to a small red circle that marked the position of the camp, "and we're heading for here."

He slid his finger towards the coast. "It's about 200 kilometres away. The GPS stations are on Ninnis Glacier.

Do you know who the Ninnis Glacier is named after?"

Lucy shook her head.

"Belgrave Ninnis," announced Doug.

"What a cool name!" exclaimed Lucy. "Who was he?"

"One of Douglas Mawson's men, of course," said Doug, smiling.

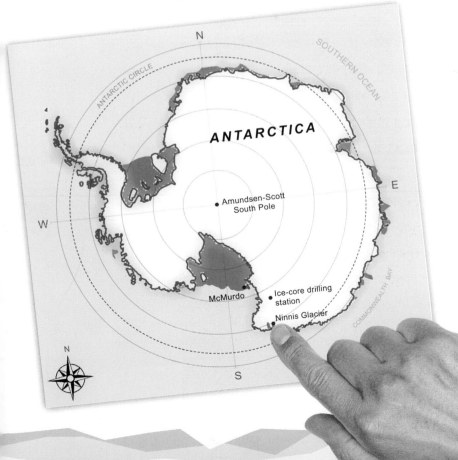

The next morning, Lucy, Doug and Andy set out on three snowmobiles, with Doug's machine pulling a sledge stacked with equipment. They had everything they would need for a week out on the ice with them, including plenty of spare food and fuel in case they were caught out by bad weather.

"Good luck!" called Paul, as he waved them off.

Lucy revved up her snowmobile and followed Doug. Andy followed her. After a few minutes, Lucy glanced backwards. The tents of the drilling camp already looked like tiny yellow specks on the horizon.

Nothing lay ahead of them except hundreds of kilometres of icy landscape.

After a whole day's driving, with just a short stop for lunch, Doug brought his snowmobile to a halt. Lucy and Andy stopped beside him and turned off their engines.

"We'll stop here for the night," announced Doug. "Let's get the tents off the sledge."

They put up their tents and then parked the snowmobiles facing into the wind.

"That'll stop any snow building up against them," Doug said.

Before they went to sleep that night, Doug told Lucy more about Douglas Mawson.

"Mawson first came to Antarctica with Ernest Shackleton in 1907," he said. "On that expedition, the team travelled more than 1,600 kilometres over the ice sheet. Amazingly, they hauled their own sledges all the way."

"He came back in 1911," Doug continued. "Then Mawson organised his own trip – the Australasian Antarctic Expedition. His men built a hut at Commonwealth Bay to live and work in. It's on the coast about 300 kilometres from here. For three years, Mawson studied the rocks, the glaciers, the wildlife, the weather, the…"

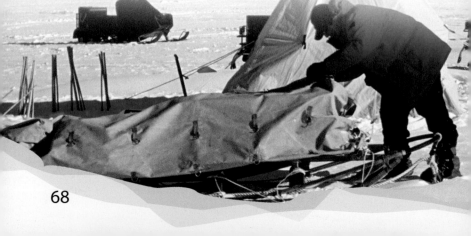

Andy interrupted. "Okay, Doug. Enough about Mawson!" he said, laughing. "Let's get some sleep."

The trio travelled the whole of the next day and set up camp again. In the morning of the following day, they closed in on the first GPS station.

"I've put the exact positions of the stations as waypoints in our GPS unit," said Doug. "The GPS should take us right to them."

The GPS worked perfectly. They arrived at the first GPS station, where Andy ran some checks.

"Looks like the solar panel has failed," he explained. "We've got a replacement on the sledge."

THE SNOW SPORTS CATALOGUE

Travel around the Antarctic in comfort and style with our state-of-the-art transportation devices. Don't let the harsh and treacherous conditions get the better of you; let us help keep you safe and sound.

TWIN OTTER PLANE

Ensure safe transportation of yourself and your equipment by travelling in the Twin Otter aircraft. This high-wing, twin-engine plane has been designed with remote and dangerous environments in mind, making it strong and reliable in even the harshest of weather conditions. The Twin Otter is well equipped with both wheels and skis, enabling it to take off safely and land anywhere. With a maximum speed of 290 kph (180 mph), the Twin Otter will get you where you want to be faster than you can say 'penguin'!

SNOWMOBILE XT80

This land vehicle provides explorers with a speedy and fun way of zipping around the Antarctic landscape. Getting you close to nature, this vehicle provides a safe and exciting way for you to experience the snowy continent. It has the ability to move smoothly at speeds of up to 70 kph (43 mph), zipping across unstable ground with ease. The skis at the front of the vehicle provide you with superb directional control and precision when navigating over snow and ice.

FROSTNIP CROSS-COUNTRY SKIS

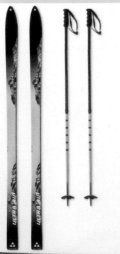

Frostnip cross-country skis are the premier products for the modern intrepid explorer. Expertly crafted and using the latest in snow-travel technology, these skis are a must-have for any adventurer. The core of the skis is made from a dense maple wood, with tips made of a lighter aspen. This makes the skis lightweight, so steering on ice and snow is easy.

ICE-CORE DRILLING

Since Antarctica remains icy throughout the year, snow that falls does not melt away and disappear. Instead, it builds up over thousands of years and forms solid ice. This ice can provide many clues about what the climate was like thousands of years ago.

Firn
The top layer consists of firn, which is snow that has partially melted, refrozen and become dense from the pressure of the snow above it. It takes about two years to form.

Readings taken from Vostok Station

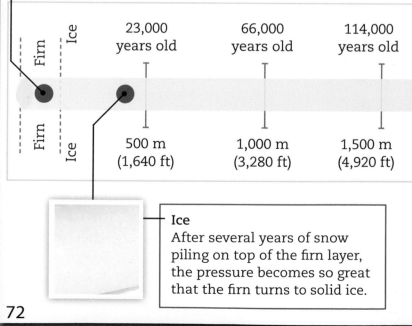

Firn	Ice	23,000 years old	66,000 years old	114,000 years old

Firn	Ice	500 m (1,640 ft)	1,000 m (3,280 ft)	1,500 m (4,920 ft)

Ice
After several years of snow piling on top of the firn layer, the pressure becomes so great that the firn turns to solid ice.

ICE CORES AND CLIMATE CHANGE

By examining which elements were in the air and in what quantities, scientists can determine how warm the Earth was in the past. They can then figure out whether the Earth is getting warmer. By studying climate-change patterns, they can also predict how the climate might change in the future.

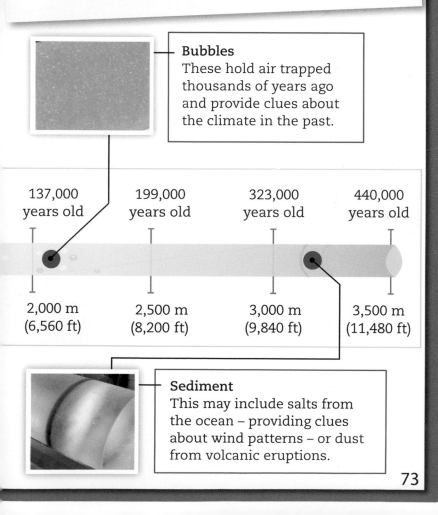

Bubbles
These hold air trapped thousands of years ago and provide clues about the climate in the past.

137,000 years old	199,000 years old	323,000 years old	440,000 years old
2,000 m (6,560 ft)	2,500 m (8,200 ft)	3,000 m (9,840 ft)	3,500 m (11,480 ft)

Sediment
This may include salts from the ocean – providing clues about wind patterns – or dust from volcanic eruptions.

73

CHAPTER 5

"All done. The solar panel's working now," called Andy to the others.

"Good work, Andy," said Doug. "We should rope up before we go on. We'll be on the Ninnis Glacier soon, and there will be some crevasses. Can you remember what to do from your training, Lucy?"

"Yes, I think so," Lucy replied.

Using strong steel cables, they connected the snowmobiles and sledges together, with a gap of about 10 metres between each one. Then they put on climbing harnesses and roped themselves up to the snowmobiles.

"All ready?" called Doug. "Keep your eyes peeled and your speed down."

With a loud buzz, the snowmobiles came to life, and they ventured out onto the glacier, heading for the next GPS station.

Lucy was nervous – she felt very small in this vast landscape – but after a few minutes, she began to enjoy the ride. She thought about what it must have been like for explorers like Mawson to haul a heavy sledge without a snowmobile or dog team.

Suddenly, she was woken from her daydreaming. Doug had stopped his snowmobile and was waving frantically at her. A split second later, Lucy felt herself falling! She had hit a crevasse….

Slowly, Lucy opened her eyes. She was dangling in mid-air, and her heart was pounding. The sledge hung a few metres away on its wire cable, with her snowmobile beneath it. Lucy looked down and quickly wished that she hadn't. All she could see below were the dark depths of the crevasse. She couldn't see the bottom, just icy blackness stretching away.

"Lucy! Lucy! Are you all right?" It was Doug's voice. She looked up again. He was peering over the lip of the crevasse.

She called back, "I'm fine… I think."

"Phew! Hold on for a couple of minutes, and we'll haul you out."

Quickly, Doug and Andy set up a pulley system on the rope, and soon Lucy was clambering out of the crevasse. She was still shaking.

"That was scary," she declared, with a small smile.

"Now for your snowmobile and the sledge," said Doug.

The plan was to use the other two snowmobiles to haul Lucy's snowmobile and the sledge back out of the crevasse, but the skis slipped and slithered on the ice as they revved the snowmobiles' engines. They struggled for more than an hour.

"It's no good," Doug said, grimly. "Let's give up."

They lowered Doug into the crevasse to retrieve as much equipment as he could from the sledge.

"I've got one tent, the sleeping bags and some food," he said, as he clambered to the surface. "It's not much, but it's better than nothing. Now stand well clear."

He released the cables. For a few seconds, there was silence. Then they heard a muffled crash as the snowmobile and sledge smashed into the bottom of the crevasse. The silence returned. Lucy, Doug and Andy stood and looked at each other.

"Now what do we do?" said Lucy.

"We have to get back to camp as fast as we can," replied Doug.

"We've got enough stuff to survive for a few days," said Andy, as he collected up the remaining equipment. "We can all squeeze into one tent, we have plenty of fuel and food and Lucy can travel on my snowmobile. So it's not all bad news."

A sudden gust of wind ruffled their anoraks. Lucy shivered.

"Looks like the weather's closing in," said Doug ominously, as he stared up at the sky.

"Let's get that tent up, have something to eat and get ourselves warm," said Doug, more cheerfully.

By the time the tent was up, the wind was blowing fiercely. Lucy peeped out of the door. "It's starting to snow," she said to Andy, filled with apprehension.

"I've radioed McMurdo," said Doug, "so they know we're returning to camp. The batteries in our GPS are dead, though, so I couldn't tell McMurdo exactly where we are."

"Haven't we got some spare batteries?" asked Andy.

"Yes, but they're on the sledge…," Doug continued, "at the bottom of the crevasse. Search planes can't fly in these conditions anyway, so we'll just have to stay put for a while."

That night, the wind grew steadily stronger, and the snow grew steadily heavier. Lucy tried desperately to sleep, but the wind was howling and shrieking outside, making the tent's fabric flap around violently and making Lucy ever more uneasy.

Doug saw the worried look on Lucy's face. "Don't worry, Lucy. The tent can take it. We won't get blown away!"

But the blizzard carried on raging for the whole night, and it was still raging the next day. Lucy was beginning to worry that they might run out of food before the storm ran out of juice – or before a team from McMurdo could find them.

As they sheltered in the tent the next day, Lucy, trying to distract herself, asked Doug to tell her more about Douglas Mawson's expedition in Antarctica.

"Oh, Lucy!" exclaimed Andy, sticking his fingers in his ears. "Not more about Mawson. As if things weren't bad enough!"

Doug grinned. "Mawson set out from his base to make maps of this part of Antarctica," he explained, showing Lucy a photo and some stamps of Mawson from his personal collection. "He took two men with him – Belgrave Ninnis and Xavier Mertz. They must have been quite close to where we are now when Ninnis fell into a crevasse, taking his sledge and dog team with him. All that Mawson and Mertz could see were two injured dogs, lying on an icy shelf about 45 metres down. Ninnis and his sledge had disappeared."

"Did they get him out?" asked Lucy.

"No. They couldn't. They had to leave him."

"That's terrible. So that's why this place is called Ninnis Glacier?" whispered Lucy.

Doug went on. "Worse still, nearly all their food, and all the dog food, was on Ninnis's sledge – all gone. Mawson and Mertz were weeks away from base – and in desperate trouble."

MAWSON'S DIARY

The diary entry below includes a description of the disappearance of Ninnis. It is taken from Mawson's own account of the expedition, *Home of the Blizzard*, which was published in 1915.

14 December, 1912

A light east-south-east wind was blowing as the sledges started away eastwards this morning. The weather was sunny, and the temperature registered -6 degrees C. Everything was, for once, in harmony, and the time was at hand when we should turn our faces homewards.

Mertz was well in advance of us when I noticed him hold up his ski stick and then go on. This was a signal for something unusual, so I looked out for crevasses or some other explanation of his action. On reaching the spot where Mertz had signalled and seeing no sign of any irregularity, I jumped onto the sledge. Glancing at the ground a moment after, I noticed the faint indication of a crevasse. I turned quickly round, called out a warning word to Ninnis, and then dismissed it from my thoughts.

Then there was no sound from behind except a faint, plaintive whine from one of the dogs. When I next looked back, it was in response to the anxious gaze of Mertz, who had turned round and halted in his tracks. Behind me, nothing met the eye but my own sledge tracks running back in the distance.

Where were Ninnis
and his sledge?

The lid of a crevasse
had broken in; two sledge
tracks led up to it on
the far side, but only
one continued on the
other side.

Lieutenant B.E.S. Ninnis, R.F.

I leaned over and shouted into the dark depths
below. No sound came back but the moaning of
a dog, caught on a shelf just visible 45 metres below.
Close by was what appeared in the gloom to be the
remains of the tent and a canvas tank containing
food for three men for a fortnight.

We broke back the edge of the névé (glacial snow)
lid and took turns leaning over, secured by a rope,
and calling into the darkness in the hope that our
companion might still be alive. For three hours
we called unceasingly, but no answering sound
came back. We felt that there was little hope.

In such moments, action is the only tolerable thing.
Stricken dumb with the pity of it and heavy of
heart, we turned our minds mechanically to what
lay nearest at hand.

POLES APART:
FINDING THE SOUTH POLE

South Magnetic Pole: this is what the south needle on a compass points to. Think of the Earth as a giant magnet. The ends of this magnet with the strongest forces are the poles, which pull on the compass's needle. What makes the Earth magnetic is its fluid core. Because the fluid is constantly moving, the magnetic poles don't stay in the same places.

Geographic South Pole: this is at the southernmost point of the Earth. Imagine if there were a long stick stuck all the way through the planet at its axis – the point from which the Earth spins. This stick would therefore poke out at the Earth's Geographic North and South Poles.

Ceremonial South Pole: located a short distance from the Geographic South Pole, the Ceremonial Pole is where explorers can get their photographs taken at the end of their journey. It is marked by a red-and-white-striped pole and is surrounded by flags of the Antarctic Treaty signatory countries.

The Antarctic Treaty is an agreement between 50 countries, which decided that Antarctica should be a protected area where scientific research has priority.

Pole locations

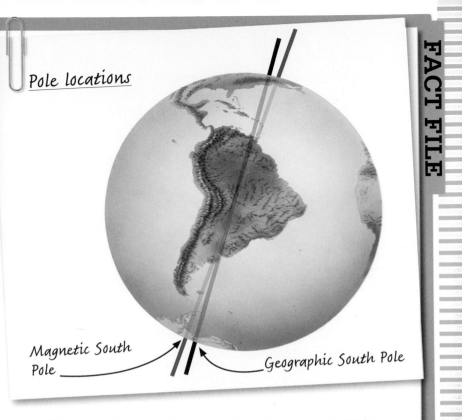

Magnetic South Pole

Geographic South Pole

Shifting ice: the marker for the Geographic Pole is situated on a moving sheet of ice that is more than 3.2 km (2 miles) thick. This sheet drifts about 10 m (30 ft) per year. This means that new markers need to be placed on the correct site once every year. Below are examples of a few of the markers at the Poles.

Geographic, 2011   Geographic, 2012   Ceremonial

RACE TO THE POLE!
AMUNDSEN VS SCOTT

AMUNDSEN

Departure from base camp at the Bay of Whales
20 October, 1911

782 km (486 miles) to the Pole
9 November, 1911

1,005 km (624 miles) to the Pole
31 October, 1911

Arrival in the Antarctic
14 January, 1911

782 km (486 miles) to the Pole
23 November, 1911

1,005 km (624 miles) to the Pole
9 November, 1911

SCOTT

Arrival in the Antarctic
4 January, 1911

Departure from base camp at Cape Evans
1 November, 1911

In 1911, two explorers – Robert Falcon Scott and Roald Amundsen – set out to attempt to be the first person to reach the South Pole. It was a fierce competition, but in the end, Amundsen won. Amundsen, a Norwegian, was an experienced polar traveller, having lived in the Arctic for several years. Many believe this was the secret of his success.

558 km (347 miles)
to the Pole
17 November, 1911

181 km (112 miles)
to the Pole
7 December, 1911

SOUTH POLE

558 km (347 miles)
to the Pole
21 December, 1911

181 km (112 miles)
to the Pole – the
southernmost point
reached by Ernest
Shackleton in 1909
9 January, 1912

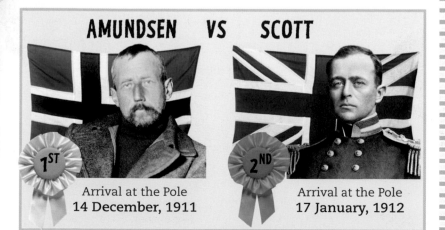

AMUNDSEN VS SCOTT

1ST
Arrival at the Pole
14 December, 1911

2ND
Arrival at the Pole
17 January, 1912

CHAPTER 6

Lucy was exhausted from the previous night's restlessness and slept for most of the following afternoon. When she woke up, Andy and Doug were not in the tent. She could hear them talking outside. She clambered out of her sleeping bag, put on her anorak and went to join them. The wind had died down, and the snow had stopped, but there was low cloud all around. She could just about see Andy and Doug, but everything else looked white. She couldn't tell where the land stopped and the sky started.

"This is what we call a white-out," said Andy.

"We're leaving as soon as we can," said Doug, brushing snow off his snowmobile with his arm.

"Are we going back?" asked Lucy.

Andy answered. "No. We might get lost. We should head for the coast. It'll be much easier for a rescue team to pick us up down there. Actually, Doug thinks we should head for Commonwealth Bay, where Mawson's base was. Mawson's hut is still there, if we can find it."

"How are we going to find the way without a GPS?" asked Lucy.

"Simple. The old-fashioned way – with a map and a compass," answered Doug.

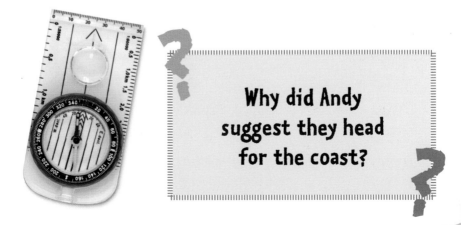

Why did Andy suggest they head for the coast?

"Aren't we too close to the South Magnetic Pole to use a compass accurately?" asked Lucy.

Lucy knew that the south end of a compass needle always points to the South Magnetic Pole. Because the pole was only a few hundred kilometres away, the needle of their compass would slowly move around even if they travelled in a straight line.

"You're right," agreed Andy, "but we'll just have to do the best we can. We don't really have a choice."

"How far is Mawson's hut?"

"Doug thinks it's about 95 kilometres away, but it'll be slow going in these white-out conditions. The ice could be bumpy, and we've got another glacier to cross. It'll probably take us at least 12 hours to get there – if we can stay awake."

Doug led the way, using his compass to guide them.

It was hard going. In the white-out, Lucy couldn't see a thing except the snowmobile and Andy. She had no idea where she was. Suddenly, the snowmobile ground to a halt. Doug was standing and staring at a mound in the snow, about one-metre high. He gave it a kick.

"Ouch!" he said. "There's something hard in here."

"Let's dig it out," said Andy. "The exercise will warm us up a bit."

Lucy, Doug and Andy quickly began to scrape the snow away with their hands and a ski pole. Bit by bit, part of a wooden frame appeared.

"It looks like an old sledge!" exclaimed Lucy.

"Wow! I think you're right," said Andy.

They cleared away more snow.

"That's strange," said Andy. "It's only half a sledge – the back half, by the look of it. I wonder where the front half is."

"Have you ever seen anything like this, Doug?" asked Lucy.

Doug didn't answer. Lucy and Andy turned around and looked at him.

Doug was sitting perfectly still, staring at the sledge in amazement.

"It's Mawson's sledge," he muttered. "It's Douglas Mawson's sledge."

"It can't be," said Andy. "Mawson was here more than a hundred years ago. Surely, if it was his sledge, it would be buried deep in the ice by now."

"I know. It seems impossible, but it must be Mawson's sledge. Let me tell you why."

"After Ninnis fell into the glacier, Mawson and Mertz tried to get back to their base," explained Doug. "The poor dogs had nothing to eat, and they became weaker and weaker as they pulled the sledge. One by one, they died. Mawson and Mertz were so short on food that they had to eat the dogs. Gradually, they became weaker too because they had to pull the sledge themselves. They threw away the heavy equipment to make the sledge lighter, including Mawson's precious camera and films."

"Mertz became very ill and got badly frostbitten. In the end, he couldn't go on. Mawson put him on the sledge and hauled the sledge alone, but Mertz died. Mawson buried him in the snow. He was exhausted and feeling ill too, but he kept going alone. So what do you think Mawson did to make things easier for himself?" Doug asked Lucy and Andy.

In a flash, Andy realised what Doug meant.

"He cut his sledge in half to save weight, didn't he?" he replied quietly.

"Exactly," said Doug, "and this must be the half he left behind."

Doug told the others how Mawson cut the heavy sledge in half using his small pocketknife. It was an astonishing story.

"That must have taken hours!" commented Lucy, amazed.

"It probably did," said Doug. "He took the front end of the sledge and abandoned the back end here. Do you believe me now?"

"I think I do," said Lucy.

"If you think that's weird, take a look at this," said Andy. He pointed to the ground on the other side of the sledge. Doug's eyes opened even wider. Leading away from them were sledge tracks in the snow."

"These are fresh tracks," said Doug, looking closely at them.

"But who could have made them?" asked Lucy, puzzled. "Nobody has been here."

"It was Mawson," whispered Doug. "These are the tracks of Douglas Mawson's sledge."

"They can't be, Doug!" said Andy. "That was more than a century ago.

Your mind is playing tricks on you. It must be the lack of sleep."

"Come on!" Doug cried, ignoring Andy. "Let's follow them. Mawson is leading us to safety!"

Lucy and Andy looked at each other, eyebrows raised.

"It's official," said Andy slowly, shaking his head. "Doug has gone crazy!"

NAVIGATION GAME

Navigating around Antarctica in the snow is not always an easy task. This means that being able to use a compass is essential for finding your way around. Use the compass and follow the directions to take a tour of Antarctica. With some practice, you will no longer be a navigating novice but will learn how to be captain of the compass!

Answers:
1. two south, one east. 2. two south, eight west. 3. two east, four north. 4. two east, one south, three east, one north.

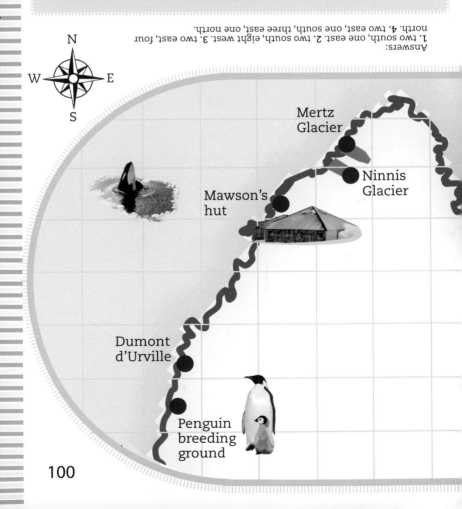

Mertz Glacier

Ninnis Glacier

Mawson's hut

Dumont d'Urville

Penguin breeding ground

Start at McMurdo and look for the red dots. Work out how many squares you need to move and write the numbers in the spaces below.

1. Time for work! Travel south __ square(s) and east __ square(s) to reach the ice-core-drilling station.
2. Work's finished, and it's penguin breeding time! Travel __ square(s) south and __ square(s) west to see the penguin chicks.
3. One last stop before heading home – go __ square(s) east and __ square(s) north to visit Mawson's Hut.
4. Phew! What a long trip! Can you work out how to get back to McMurdo?

Tip: Avoid the icy water!

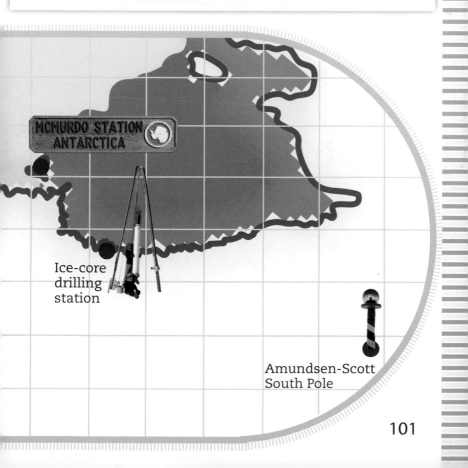

Ice-core drilling station

Amundsen-Scott South Pole

MAKE YOUR OWN COMPASS

If you'd like to try finding your way using a compass, you can make one of your own with a few simple materials.

WHAT YOU WILL NEED:

- large sewing needle
- magnet
- knife
- cork
- permanent-ink marker
- bowl

1 With the hole, or eye, of the needle pointing downwards, stroke the magnet along the needle.

2 Using a knife, carefully slice a piece of cork.

3 Push the point of the magnetised needle through the sliced cork. Be careful!

4 Draw an arrow on the cork towards the point of the needle. This is your north point. Draw dots around the cork to show east, south and west.

5 Half-fill a bowl with water and place it on a flat surface. Float the cork on the water. When the water has settled, the point of the needle will swing around to point north.

FACT:

A magnet will always point north and south, which is why, if you were standing between the Geographic South Pole and the South Magnetic Pole, your compass would point in the wrong direction.

GROUND-TO-AIR SIGNALS

If you get stuck out in the middle of Antarctica, you'll need to find ways to communicate with planes and helicopters overhead. Here are some ground signals you can make using stones.

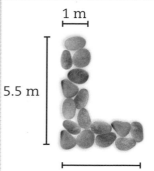

1 m

5.5 m

3.5 m

1 m

Letter height:
1 m (3 ft) wide by
5.5 m (18 ft) high

Letter width:
3.5 m (12 ft) wide
by 1 m (3 ft) high

Require doctor – serious injuries

Aircraft badly damaged

Require medical supplies

Will attempt to take off

Not understood

Require engineer

Unable to proceed

Probably safe
to land here

Require food
and water

Indicate direction
to proceed

Going in this
direction

All well

Require food
and oil

No – negative

Require compass
and map

Require signal
lamp

Yes – affirmative

CHAPTER 7

"These tracks lead in the right direction, so we may as well follow them," said Doug. "It's almost impossible to navigate with a compass in this white-out."

They pushed on, inching through the whiteness.

Suddenly, Doug stopped his snowmobile. Andy nearly drove into the back of it.

"Look!" said Doug, pointing at the ground.

Lying under a dusting of snow was a large metal can. Doug scraped the snow off and sniffed it. "Smells like paraffin," he said, handing the can to Andy. "They used paraffin fuel in camping stoves in Mawson's time."

Andy examined it. Apart from a few scratches, the can looked new. Then Lucy noticed the corner of a piece of paper sticking out of the snow. She shook the snow off it. It was a box and written on its wrapper was the word 'Pemmican'.

"This stuff is from Mawson's time, but it looks as if somebody dropped it here a few hours ago!" said Doug, excitedly.

"This is getting weirder and weirder," muttered Lucy. She felt goosebumps running up her back – and it wasn't from the cold.

"I'm officially spooked!" added Andy.

Shortly afterwards, the tracks led them into another area of crevasses, and they stopped again.

"This must be Mertz Glacier," said Doug.

"Mawson named it after Xavier Mertz. We need to rope up for a while."

On and on they went. Lucy was wearing several layers of clothes, but she still began to feel cold. When Andy turned around to make sure she was okay, he could see her shivering. He stopped the snowmobile.

"Lucy," he said, "are you okay?"

"I feel… really… freezing," murmured Lucy.

"I think she's getting hypothermic," said Doug. He recognised the signs that showed that Lucy's body temperature was falling dangerously low. "Quick, Andy, let's get the tent up and get her into a sleeping bag."

A little while later, Lucy was sitting in the tent, sipping a warm cup of tea.

"Feeling better?" asked Doug, looking up from the map he was studying. "At least you've stopped shivering."

Lucy nodded. "How much farther do we have to go?" she asked.

"I'd estimate it's only about five kilometres," he replied. "The weather has gone downhill again, though, so we might have to camp here."

"Doug," said Andy quietly, "did Mawson make it back to his hut?"

Doug chuckled. "So all of a sudden you're interested in Mawson, are you?" he exclaimed.

"Okay, very funny," said Andy. "It's just that, if those tracks, the fuel can and the pemmican wrapper are really Mawson's, I'd like to know what happened to him."

"Well," said Doug, showing them some more photos of Mawson, "after Mertz died, Mawson didn't think he had much chance of survival, but he soldiered on. He figured that even if he did get back to the hut alive, his ship the *Aurora*, and all his men would have left, because winter was setting in."

"Then Mawson also stumbled into a crevasse. He was left dangling on a rope, just as you were, Lucy. With incredible willpower, he pulled himself up the rope to the surface. Then he slipped back into the crevasse and had to climb up all over again."

"He carried on for twenty days, with almost

no food, getting slower and slower. Just when he thought he couldn't go any further, he found a stash of food. It had been left for him by a search party from his base. The food saved his life."

27c

AUSTRALIAN
ANTARCTIC
TERRITORY

Sir Douglas Mawson Centenary—1982

"It was only another 40 kilometres to the hut," continued Doug, "but it took Mawson 10 days to get there."

"Was the *Aurora* still there?" asked Lucy.

"No. It had left just 5 hours before Mawson arrived. He thought he was stranded in Antarctica. Then he saw figures moving around outside the hut. A small team of men had stayed behind in case Mawson, Mertz and Ninnis got back. So he was safe. It was one of the most incredible feats of survival in the history of the Antarctic," said Doug.

They sat silently for a few minutes.

"Anyway, we need to think about our survival now," announced Doug. "I think we should try to reach the hut, whatever the weather. Otherwise, we could be here for days, and we're running out of food and fuel."

"I agree," said Andy.

"Me too," said Lucy confidently, although inside she was terrified.

They packed up the tent and got back on the snowmobiles.

"There's somebody ahead!" cried Andy, suddenly. They all stared into the falling snow, blinking.

For a split second, they glimpsed a faint figure. Then it was gone.

"Mawson," gasped Lucy. "I wonder if that was…Douglas Mawson."

An hour later, Lucy saw something taking shape in the distance. "There it is!" she shouted, pointing ahead of the snowmobile.

Mawson's wooden hut loomed out of the snow. The tracks they had been following stopped just outside the door. Lucy, Andy and Doug jumped off their snowmobiles. Andy pushed open the door. Snow swirled around him as he stumbled in, followed by Lucy and Doug.

The three of them stood and stared. The hut was still full of old equipment that Mawson and his men had used. There were cans of food, bottles of sauce, plates, books, tables and chairs and bits and pieces of clothing.

"Amazing," said Doug, looking around. "I've always wanted to see this."

"Let's get the sleeping bags and the stove inside," said Andy. "I'll radio McMurdo and tell them we're here."

Lucy went out to collect their gear from the snowmobile.

She shouted for Andy and Doug to join her. "Look," she said, pointing at the ground, "the tracks we followed have disappeared."

Again, they caught sight of the faint figure. They watched as it walked away from the hut and disappeared into the snow.

"Thanks, Douglas!" shouted Doug.

THE MIDNIGHT SUN

Here are some examples of what explorers would have eaten in the early 1900s and what modern-day explorers would eat on expeditions nowadays.

◇ ◇ ◇ MENU ◇ ◇ ◇

The Midnight Sun is a brand-new café catering to the needs of Antarctic explorers. Our menu offers high-energy meals and snacks 24 hours a day.

BREAKFAST AND SNACKS

Pemmican (e)
Dried beef mixed with lard and berries

Wholemeal crackers (e)
Served with butter

~~~~~~

LUNCH AND DINNER

Hoosh (e)
Stew of wholemeal crackers, pemmican and snow

~~~~~~

DRINKS

Tea
Hot cocoa
Both served with dried milk and sugar

~~~~~~

DESSERT

Chocolate (e)
Bar of semi-sweet chocolate

e = high-energy food

MENU

It's been more than a hundred years, but the Midnight Sun is still providing polar explorers with all the high-energy food they need.

BREAKFAST AND SNACKS

Crackers (e)
Served with butter, cheese, peanut butter or apricot jam

Dried-fruit salad (e)
With apples and apricots

Assorted nuts (e)

Muesli or muesli bars (e)
Served with dried milk powder mixed with water

DRINKS

Tea

Hot cocoa

Instant coffee

All served with dried milk and sugar

e = high-energy food

LUNCH AND DINNER

Noodle soup
Made from dried noodles and available in tomato and basil, chicken or vegetable

Salmon (e)
Freeze-dried and served with your choice of peas and carrots, peas and corn or green beans

Leg of ham (e)
From a can and served with potatoes and onions

Pasta (e)
With pesto, mushroom and bacon or sour cream and chive sauce

Tuna (e)
Freeze-dried and served with rice or noodles

DESSERT

Chocolate (e)
Dark, milk or with peanuts

GHOSTS OF ANTARCTICA

There are many ghost stories about Antarctica. Some people say that it is the most haunted place on Earth. This is because it has more abandoned settlements than anywhere else. Would you want to visit any of these haunted places?

SCOTT'S HUT

Thanks to the cold, everything in Captain Scott's hut has been frozen in time, and items from the 1910s have been left exactly as they were. Scott and two others died on their way back to the hut in 1912. Since then, voices and footsteps have been heard in the cabin.

GRYTVIKEN

The Sub-Antarctic island of South Georgia was home to at least seven whaling communities at the beginning of the twentieth century. The most spectacular was Grytviken, which was founded in 1904. It is the final resting place of Ernest Shackleton but was abandoned in 1966. Its church remains as an eerie reminder of the thriving village it once was.

OUR LADY OF THE SNOWS

This shrine commemorates petty officer Richard T. Williams. He was killed on 6 January, 1956, when the tractor he was driving broke through the ice off Cape Royds and fell to the bottom of McMurdo Sound. His body was never found, but Our Lady of the Snows was built in 1957 in his memory.

HEKTOR WHALING STATION

Deception Island is home to Hektor, one of the oldest ghost towns in Antarctica. It was built in 1912 as a whaling outpost. It was abandoned in 1931 and has been left untouched ever since. A cemetery and the tombs of thirty-five men were buried by a volcanic eruption in 1969.

THE TRUTH BEHIND THE TALES

Ghost sightings in Antarctica may actually be hallucinations. In the summertime in Antarctica, the sun never sets. This makes it difficult for some people to sleep, so they suffer from sleep deprivation (see p. 58), which causes hallucinations.

EPILOGUE

Lucy, Andy and Doug were exhausted after their long journey. They crawled into their sleeping bags and fell asleep.

A few hours later, Lucy woke up. Doug was already awake.

"The weather's cleared," he said.

Lucy stepped outside. The wind had stopped, and the sky was cloudless and blue.

Doug joined her.

"There's a research ship in the bay. Its helicopter will be here in an hour to pick us up."

Lucy let out a sigh of relief.

A month later, Lucy was back at McMurdo Station, on board a flight bound for New

Zealand. She thought about her adventure with Doug and Andy. In the comfort and safety of the plane, she was sure that they must have imagined Mawson's tracks and the faint figure in the snow. After all, they were very tired at the time, but would they have survived without Mawson's help?

As the plane climbed into the air, Lucy took a small parcel out of her pocket. Doug had given it to her as a leaving present. She unwrapped it slowly and almost jumped out of her seat. It was the pemmican box she had found in the snow! Along the edge were the words 'Australasian Antarctic Expedition, 1911'.

Lucy couldn't believe her eyes. It seemed impossible, but perhaps Mawson had truly been helping them after all!

ANTARCTIC QUIZ

See if you can remember the answers to these questions about what you have read.

1. What does MICE stand for?

2. What is the name of Antarctica's biggest research base?

3. Who, in Doug's opinion, is the greatest Antarctic hero?

4. Who was the first person to reach the South Pole?

5. What site does Lucy visit at Cape Evans?

6. Which is the largest species of penguin?

7. Which vehicles are the 'workhorses' of Antarctica?

8. According to Andy, how long ago did ice that is buried 300 metres below the surface fall?

9. What can air bubbles in an ice core tell scientists?

10. What will studying ice cores tell the team about ancient volcanoes?

11. What ailment can hallucinations be a symptom of?

12. In what year did Douglas Mawson's Australasian Antarctic Expedition take place?

13. Which two men did Douglas Mawson take with him on his expedition?

14. Where does Doug suggest the team go during the white-out?

15. What objects do the team find buried in the snow?

Answers on page 125.

GLOSSARY

Acclimatise
To get used to a particular climate.

Auger
A drill used for making holes in the ground.

Chic
Very fashionable.

Deprivation
Not having enough, or any, of something essential.

Diabetes
A disease in which a person's body cannot control the amount of sugar in it.

GPS (Global Positioning System)
A system that provides location and time information using satellites.

Hallucination
Something imagined.

Insulating
Keeping in warmth.

Intrepid
Fearless and adventurous.

Plaintive
Sounding sad.

Precipitation
Rainfall or snowfall.

INDEX

Answers to the Antarctic Quiz:
1. Multinational Ice Core Project; **2.** McMurdo Station; **3.** Douglas Mawson; **4.** Roald Amundsen; **5.** Scott's Hut; **6.** Emperor; **7.** Twin Otters; **8.** 10,000 years ago; **9.** What the Earth's climate was like in the past; **10.** When ancient volcanoes erupted in Antarctica; **11.** Sleep deprivation; **12.** 1911; **13.** Belgrave Ninnis and Xavier Mertz; **14.** Mawson's hut; **15.** Half of a sledge, a fuel can and a pemmican box.

Guide for Parents

DK Reads is a three-level interactive reading adventure series for children, developing the habit of reading widely for both pleasure and information. These chapter books have an exciting main narrative interspersed with a range of reading genres to suit your child's reading ability, as required by the National Curriculum. Each book is designed to develop your child's reading skills, fluency, grammar awareness and comprehension in order to build confidence and engagement when reading.

Ready for a *Reading Alone* book

YOUR CHILD SHOULD

- be able to read independently and silently for extended periods of time.
- read aloud flexibly and fluently, in expressive phrases with the listener in mind.
- respond to what they are reading with an enquiring mind.

A VALUABLE AND SHARED READING EXPERIENCE

Supporting children when they are reading proficiently can encourage them to value reading and to view reading as an interesting, purposeful and enjoyable pastime. So here are a few tips on how to use this book with your child.

TIP 1 Reading aloud as a learning opportunity:

- if your child has already read some of the book, ask him/her to explain the earlier part briefly.
- encourage your child to read slightly slower than his/her normal silent reading speed so that the words are clear and the listener has time to absorb the information, too.

Reading aloud provides your child with practice in expressive reading and performing to a listener, as well as a chance to share his/her responses to the storyline and the information.

TIP 2 Praise, share and chat:

- encourage your child to recall specific details after each chapter.

- provide opportunities for your child to pick out interesting words and discuss what they mean.

- discuss how the author captures the reader's interest, or how effective the non-fiction layouts are.

- ask the questions provided on some pages and in the quiz. These help develop comprehension skills and awareness of the language used.

- ask if there's anything that your child would like to discover more about.

Further information can be researched in the index of other non-fiction books or on the Internet.

A FEW ADDITIONAL TIPS

- Continue to read to your child regularly to demonstrate fluency, phrasing and expression; to find out or check information; and for sharing enjoyment.

- Encourage your child to read a range of different genres, such as newspapers, poems, review articles and instructions.

- Provide opportunities for your child to read to a variety of eager listeners, such as a sibling or a grandparent.

Series consultant **Shirley Bickler** was a longtime advocate of carefully crafted, enthralling texts for young readers. Her LIFT initiative for infant teaching was the model for the National Literacy Strategy's 'Literacy Hour', and she was co-author of *Book Bands for Guided Reading* published by Reading Recovery based at the Institute of Education.

Have you read these other great books from DK?

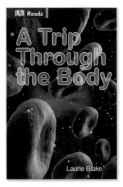

Encounter the rare animals in the mountain forests of Cambodia.

Explore the amazing systems at work inside the human body.

Step back nearly 20,000 years to the days of early cave dwellers.

Lift the bonnet on the inner workings of cars and bikes. Which team will win the race?

Be a rock detective! Unravel the clues to identify and classify the rocks.

Discover the fascinating world of creepy-crawlies in the Amazon rainforest.